SANTORINI

with a special guide to Akrotiri by
Nanno Marinatos, Dr. of archaeology

Index

Introduction	4
Visiting Santorini	16
Akrotiri - History of the Excavation	27
The Earthquake and the Eruption	30
Society and Religion	32
Relations with Crete	45
The Frescoes	47
The Pottery and Other Vessels	59
Guide to the Antiquities	63
Fira	68
The Archaeological Museum	75
Churches	76
The Convent of St. Nickolas	80
Firostefani	82
Imerovigli or Merovigli	84
Skaros - Vourvoulos - Foinikia	86
Oia	90
Coloumbos	92
Karterados - Mesaria - Monolithos	96
Episkopi Gonias	98
Kamari	102
Ancient Thera	106
Vothonas - Pyrgos	110
Profitis Ilias Monastery	112
Athinios	114
Megalochori - Akrotiri	116
Emporio	118
Perissa	122
Palaia and Nea Kameni	124
Therasia	126

ISBN 960-7310-22-5

Copyright ©:   I. Mathioulakis & Co.
Andromedas 1 - Tel.: 7661351
T.K. 162 31 Vyronas, Athens

Photographs: Theodoros Ladas, Kostas Vergas
Colour Separation: G. Papapanagopoulos & Co
Translation: David Hardy
Montaz: Dimitra Litsanidou

Introduction

There are many stories and legends about Santorini (or Thera in official language), this marvellous island of the Cyclades. These legends do not refer only to the island's history but also to the causes of its geological structure and its specific shape. There is no doubt that its gradual formation was due to the tremendous activity of local volcanos, which were also at the root of its genesis.

Thus, Santorini's soil and landscapes, the colours of the land and the sea around it, the strong light, the depth and transparency of its horizon — harmonious emerald visions — create a unique whole, the extraordinary beauty of which tends to make you forget the nightmare of its creation, and underlines the splendour of its present aspects and the fact that Santorini is recognized as the most valuable pearl in the string of the Greek archipelago. There is none who

has remained unmoved by the incomparable sight of Santorini. The vision of this island has cast its spell over people in the whole world, so that Thera is no longer a small and remote spot somewhere in the Greek seas but a focus point of interest, universally known and attracting all kinds of people — aesthetes and romantics, realists and dreamers — who ardently wish to get acquainted with it.

It is not, however, merely the grandeur and splendour of a geological phenomenon that fascinates the minds of people, but also the mystery of **Atlantis** which is identified with this island by legends and writings.

The first name of the island was **Stronghyle;** later it was known as **Calliste,** and eventually as **Thera,** a name which is said to have been given it by the son of Antesion (a Theban hero and descendant of King Cadmus), whose name was Theras. This Theras was regent of Sparta and guardian of his nephews **Procles** and **Eurysthenes**. When the boys came of age, Theras left Sparta for reasons of prestige and taking with him a group of noblemen from Orchomenos settled on the island Calliste, which was subsequently called after him Thera.

The name Santorini is evidently modern and derived from the island's church of St. Irene. Foreign seamen used to call the saint **Santa-Irini**, and in the course of time this became SANTORINI.

Millions of years ago the Greek peninsula together with the Ionian islands, the islands of the Aegean and Asia Minor formed one coherent mass of dry land. The islands of today are the outcome of unimaginably violent geological events. The natural result of these was that the sea covered with huge seismic and aeolic waves the lower parts of the new geological formation that had arisen. Santorini in particular was formed by the lava and ashes of many volcanic centres.

Initially the shape of Santorini was round, hence also its name Stronghyle, before being called Calliste. Over many centuries following its formation the local volcanos remained inactive. This long period of quiescence as well as the extremely fertile soil of volcanic origin favoured vegetation on the island, the rise of idyllic natural conditions and unique civilizations in the Mediterranean. One of these was the civilization of **Atlantis**. Ever since **Plato**, the tragic and mysterious fate of Atlantis has been retold by many writers.

Plato himself says in his dialogues **Timaeus** and **Critias** that Atlantis was a large and admirable state ruling the other islands. This «large and admirable state» exerted its power over other islands and continental strips of land between Egypt and Libya in Africa and Tyrrhenia in Europe. In the above two dialogues it is mentioned that Atlantis was a kingdom with two islands, a larger and a smaller one. Its preponderance was due to its civilization rather than to its military power. This kingdom included ten cities and of these Plato describes only two, namely, **Metropolis** and the Royal City. From the description of the shape and morphology of Metropolis it is evident that he refers to the island Stronghyle, and from that of the Royal City, that it has the characteristics of the Messara plain in Central Crete. Thus the smaller island is identified with Santorini and the larger one with Crete.

These views are supported by many authors. We would mention here in particular the archaeologist Prof. Spyros Marinatos, whose work «A Study of Symbolism in Cretomycenaean Art» refers to the wall-paintings in Amnissos, a naval yard of the Minoan empire, and the archaeologist Prof. Nicholas Platon, who maintains that Atlantis must have been Crete itself.

The main arguments put forward in support of this thesis are the following:

1. Atlantis is certainly familiar with the use of copper. The same metal, however, is also used in Crete, which is considered as the first metal-working centre of Europe.

2. Cultivation methods in Atlantis and Crete are identical. The same trees and plants mentioned by Plato as having been cultivated in Atlantis are also grown in Crete.

3. The political structure of Atlantis has great similarities with that of Minoan Crete. Both were densely populated, with people living in cities and settlements. Every city had its governor and all governors in both Atlantis and Crete were subject to royal authority. This holds particularly true for Minoan Crete, as is shown by the style of the island's palaces in different places.

4. In Atlantis, as well as in Minoan Crete, the bull was considered a sacred animal, a symbol of fertility.

5. Poseidon — the chief deity of Atlantis — is also referred to in Cretan inscriptions, where he is called P o s e i d a o n.

6. The latest excavations on Santorini prove the identity of the culture of this island with that of Minoan Crete.

Another argument in favour of identifying Minoan Crete with legendary Atlantis is the fact that Stronghyle was part of the Minoan empire.

Taking into account that Minoan Crete was almost annihilated at the time of the utter destruction of Santorini, it is most likely that Atlantis should be identified with Crete.

Plato gives us many details of the civilization of Atlantis in his writings. It is, like Minoan Crete, a wealthy and powerful state, essentially ruled by a Priest-King, with a prosperous middle class enjoying

a good life, strange shows such as bull-fights, elegant dresses, fine pottery, and various luxuries. Men and women have equal rights. All this characterized also Minoan Crete, the real Metropolis of Atlantis, a true Royal State. It has a highly developed agriculture. Its people cultivated vine, cereals, fruit trees, and other crops, while its society was wealthy and had many amenities of life, such as wonderful bathrooms, athletic grounds, and a great number of objects of high artistic and real value.

On the basis of evidence from archaeological findings underneath layers of pumice stone and ashes, the Greek historian Constantine Paparrigopoulos describes the life of the prehistoric inhabitants of Atlantis as follows: «These people were wise builders and experienced potters; they were building houses with hewn stones; to prevent destruction from earthquakes they were inserting wooden beams in the walls; they were familiar with the potter's wheel and produced vases of unusual shape and beautifully decorated. They were weaving, fishing with nets and most of their tools were made of hewn stone or obsidian. Finally, they knew the use of gold, silver, copper, tin and bronze.»

The geologist and seismologist Prof. A. Galanopoulos also writes; «For those who know, however cursorily, the great civilizations of the bronze age, there can be no doubt that Plato's Atlantis must have been a civilization of that period.» He further states: «The tremendous volcanic explosion of the former island of Stronghyle took place in Santorini at around 1500 b.C. The earthquake which accompanied the sinking of the central part of the island at the eruption of the volcano and the huge seismic wave which ensued, must have hit even the coasts of Egypt.»

We may certainly assume that this seismic wave first hit Crete with great speed reaching the island within 20-30 minutes.

Prof. Marinatos says to this effect: «Crete certainly suffered utter destruction. The coastal cities and settlements, such as Knossos, Amnissos, Nirou Chani, Mallia, Psira, Gournia, Zakro, Tylissos, Palaecastro, Aghia Triadha, Phaistos, the sacred caves, etc., were devastated within a few seconds. Only the Minoan palace of Knossos was rebuilt shortly after its destruction and continued to exist — though its power was much reduced — until about 1100 b.C. More than 83 sq.kms of land, that is about one half of the total surface of **Stronghyle** (Santorini) submerged into the sea at a depth ranging from 300 to 400 metres, creating from one moment to the other the largest **caldera** in the world.»

In order to gauge the enourmousness of this disastrous event and its consequences one should compare it with what happened at the greatest volcanic eruption of modern times, namely, that of the **Krakatoa** in the middle of the straits between **Sumatra** and **Java** in the Pacific.

In that latter case two-thirds of the surface of the island Krakatoa, i.e. some 23 sq.kms, sank into the sea to a depth of 200 to 300 metres. The caldera of Santorini has a surface which is two a half times, and a volume of about five times larger than the similar caldera of Krakatoa.

The sudden displacement of such masses of water (837.5 billion cub.m. in the case of Krakatoa, and 4,187 billion cub.m. in that of Stronghyle-Santorini) evidently caused gigantic seismic sea waves. The initial height of the «**tsunani**», as it was called, i.e. the wave of the Krakatoa eruption, was about 100m, that of Stronghyle must have been approx. 200m, and reaching the coasts of Crete it was still some 70m high.

Of what has been mentioned above one can imagine what a terrible exsplosion must have been that of the volcano of Thera, so as to account also for the destruction of Crete.

Visiting Santorini

Santorini is one of the southernmost islands of the Cyclades in the Aegean Sea. Its distance from Piraeus is 128 miles, from Iraklion (Crete) 68 miles and from Rhodes 147 miles.

The island is usually called Santorini, but its official name is **Thera**, and Thera is also called the capital of the homonymous administrative district (eparchy) in the province (nomós) of the Cyclades.

In its present form Santorini has an area of 76 sq.kms (29.4 sq. miles) and a population of 8,000. Its coast-line is 70 kms (about 143.5 miles) long. The whole group consists of the main — and largest — horseshoe-shaped island of Thera, a smaller one NE of Thera called **Therasia**, and a still smaller uninhabited islet, **Aspronísi**, in the middle of the opening of Thera's «horseshoe» towards the Aegean. In addition to these, there are three more small volcanic cone-shaped islands in the midst of the large bay, namely, **Palià Kaméni, Néa Kaméni** (with the crater of the present volcano) and **Mikri Kaméni** («Old», «New» and «Small Burnt Island»). From its northernmost tip (Cape Mavrópetra) to its southernmost end (Cape Exomyti) Thera is 18 kms or roughly 11 miles long. Its width varies between 2 to 6 kms (1.2 to 3.7 miles). The main hills are **Prophitis Elias** (556m or 1829ft), **Megalo Vounó** (353m or 1158ft)

and **Mikros Prophitis Elias** (337m or 1106ft); besides these there is a number of smaller hills.

Santorini is connected with the mainland by ship and airplane. The boats pass through the passage formed by Aspronisi at the entrance to the almost round immense caldera or bay, which has a surface of about 32 sq. miles and is 300-400m deep. One realizes immediately that here must be the crater of a gigantic ancient volcano and that the three islands around it are what remains of its walls.

At some places the cliffs rise 1150ft above sea level. They are marked by varying layers of light grey, black or dark red colour. On the top of the lowest cliff is the dazzling white string of houses and churches of the main town and the neighbouring villages.

The visitors who arrive by boat, walk or ride on mule-back a zig-zag road to the town over some 500 stairs and stair-heads. They may also use the city-bus which leaves nearby and follows another road to the town. This is what was formerly called Phirà.

A long-stretched narrow agglomeration of houses built in the typical island style, a town both simple and pleasant it is today's Thera. Shining white, clustered together, clean and well-kept dwellings and shops stand in a row, interrupted only by elegant churches and idyllic small side-streets. The picture is enlivened by the large number of donkeys patiently carrying people, merchandise and local produce.

A glorious view opens up towards the sea with its deep waters, that fill the volcanic crater, as well as towards the land with two hilltops which adorn this enchanting island. These are the hills of Prophitis Elias to the South and of Mikros Prophitis Elias to the North. Between these two rises, like a fortress, a remarkable rock — called **Monolithos** — completing the panorama of the smaller hillocks.

This beautiful landscpape is embellished by snow-white hamlets and furrowed by narrow lanes framed with gum-trees, and green spots surrounded by walls built with greenish stones. So much vegetation is surprising and, at the same time, exhilarating. The green areas are vineyards, as the soil with its grey ash content is extremely fertile and gives life to thousands of grapevines. The sea provides the necessary humidity and this is why Santorini produces such fine wines, besides tomatoes, barley, beans, yellow peas, pistachio nuts and other fruit. In addition, the island possesses a unique mineral for the production of high-quality cement (pozzolana). Popular art also flourishes on Santorini, as is shown by its home produced fine woven material, expensive embroideries and lace.

Yet Santorini seems to be under the constant threat of nature, if we remember its long history of eruptions and earthquakes. Life of man on this island is subject to unpredictable risks. But like the grapevines, which are firmly rooted in the mother soil and yield rich crops, so is also the will of its inhabitants, firm, persistent and unshakeable in their determination to continue to life on their island.

At Ancient Thera there is abundant evidence, on and under the ground, of the fact that here people lived thousands of years ago.

One of the best-known proofs of this are the remains which were uncovered at the end of the last century by the German scholar **Hiller von Gärtringen**. They are located in the NE part of the island, namely, in the ravine between the hill of Prophitis Elias and Mesa Vounó, amidst the bays of **Períssa** and **Kamári**. It is a lo-

The byzantine church at Episkopi Gonias.

cation which inspires both awe and wonder, as on one side of it you can see the imposing ruins of the ancient city, and on the other the wind-swept slopes of the ravine. And yet people continued to live here since the geometric period, i.e. about one thousand years b.C., as well as in the Ptolemaic, the Roman and the Byzantine periods.

It must have been a very important city, indeed, with temples and palaces, a basilica, an agora (market-place), a gymnasium and even a Hellenistic theatre.

Those who wish to visit Nea Kameni with its volcano will always find boats ready to bring them to the small island. There they will get on shore at a small bay surrounded by rough black slopes of cracked lava with sharp edges. The mass of the lava forms a small stony and dusty plain, with shrubs and a few fig-trees, sparsely scattered over its slopes.

On the top of Nea Kameni the crater shows that its volcano is still active, as fumes of methyl are constantly emanating from it. Yet it is with a sense of relief that the visitor will reach the top, because from there he has a splendid view of the quiet deep sea around him and of the sun-bathed cliffs of distant Thera, Therasia and Aspronisi, as well as of the tip of Oia in the NW and Akrotiri in the SW of the horseshoe of Thera.

Those who are able to visualize and interpret the history of this island with its many dramatic incidents will feel deep respect for the people who lost their lives on it, as well as for those who continue to live in this place.

The sun rises behind the neighbouring island of Anaphi and sheds its golden light on the eastern shores of the island. As the day marches on the waters of the caldera — previously under the shadow of the overtowering cliffs of Thera — begin to lie open to the golden rays of the sun which awakens them and gives them life. Then comes the moment when the sun bathes also the eastern slopes of Nea Kameni in its light, the vapours from the crater increase and — according of the laws of thermodynamics — rise in a cloud, taking on various shapes, and soon reach the town, move over to the fields and come down in the form of life-giving humidity to help the arid land bring forth its vegetation.

Santorini has a wonderful climate; though somewhat damp, it is nonetheless extremely salubrious and there have never been epidemics. The island is arid, there are no lakes nor rivers. Its inhabitants get their water supply from privately owned cisterns in which they collect rain water. There is only one spring on the island with excellent water at a location called Zoodochos (Life-giving) near Kamari.

To visit Ancient Thera one goes by car to Selladha and from there on foot to the site of the excavations. For a visit to the volcano there is, in addition to the motor-boats mentioned previously, a regular boat which leaves every afternoon. In the town the foreign visitor will ind a tourist police office, where he can obtain any useful information, and a banking office for his dealings. There is no lack of restaurants and taverns which serve good food and local («dopio») wine. For sea-bathing there are beaches at Exomyti, Períssa, Kaméni and Monólithos.

View of the village Fira capital of the island. It is a long and narrow village built in the classical style of the insular architecture, with picturesque street and simple and pleasant white-washed houses.

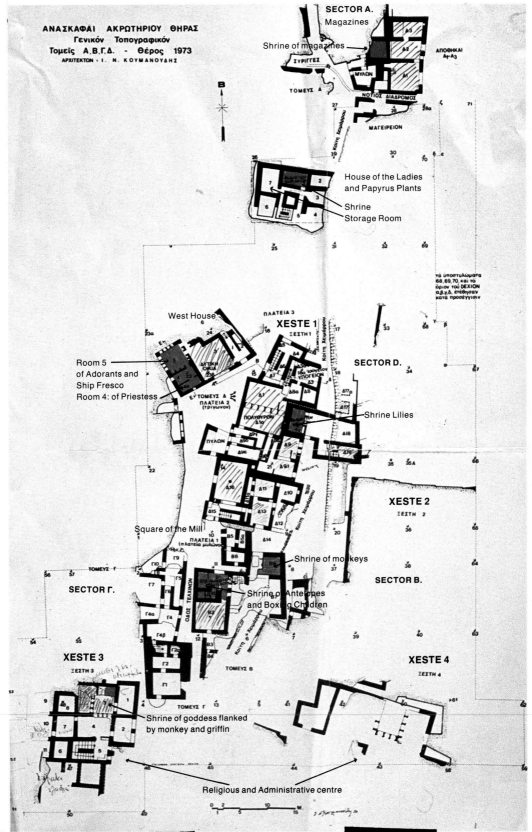

Plan of Akrotiri: The shrines are marked in red.

Akrotiri

History of the Excavation

The excavations at Akrotiri began in 1967 by Prof. Sp. Marinatos. He chose to excavate there in the hope of verifying a theory which he had formulated some thirty years ago when he was still a young man at the beginning of his career.

This theory was borne in Crete when Sp. Marinatos was digging a Minoan villa at Amnissos, the harbour-town of Knossos. While excavating, he was struck by the extent of the violence that must have been responsible for the destruction of the building. He assumed at first that an earthquake was responsible, but subsequent digging brought to light pumice, a volcanic substance. It was then that the idea occurred to him that what destroyed the villa, and in fact the palaces of Minoan Crete, was not a mere earthquake but the eruption of the volcano of Santorini. The eruption would have created huge waves (tsunamis) which would not only have hit the coastal sites of Crete, but would undoubtedly have destroyed the fleet as well. In addition, hot ash would have burned the crops. The animals would not have been able to feed, and the whole economy would have collapsed. Sp. Marinatos proceeded to publish his theory «The volcanic destruction of Minoan Crete». At that time, in the 1930ies, very few people believed it was true. Thus, he made it his goal to go to Santorini someday and try to excavate there. If he found pottery of the same period as that of the destroyed palaces and villas in Crete, he would have a confirmation of his theory.

The excavations at Akrotiri were very fruitful. What was discovered was a Minoan Pompey, the only well preserved settlement of the Bronze

1. Akrotiri: room B1 from the ground floor.

Age of about 1500 BC. The pottery found in the town is almost contemporary with that of Crete. So for many people the theory is vindicated, although not all are convinced. But the importance of the site is far greater than was expected even by the excavator. For the first time we have not only virtually intact walls and houses but whole frescoes, pottery on the places where it was left, furniture, even remnants of food. We can visualize and reconstruct the life of those people of the 16th century BC; we can also tell some things about their social organization and about their relationship with Crete.

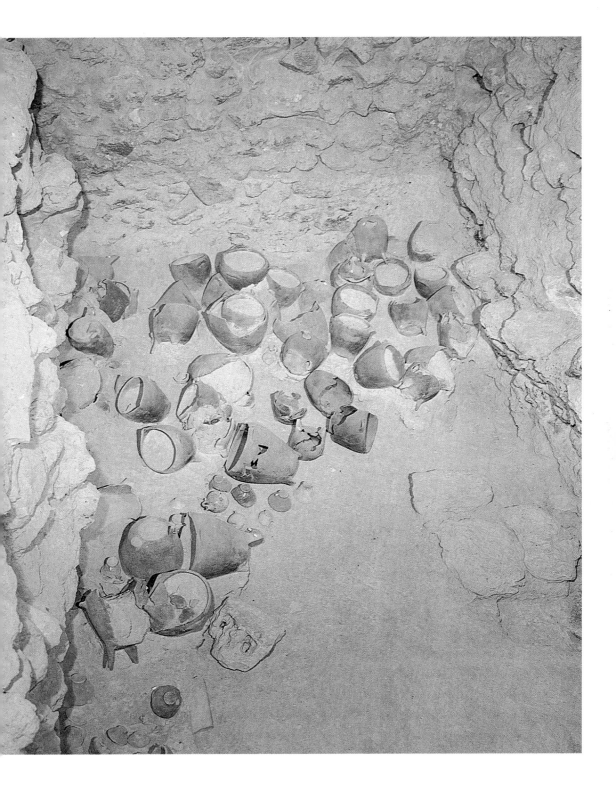

33. *The square of the West House.*

The Earthquake

and the Eruption

What we can infer from the archaeological evidence about the eruption is very interesting. We can tell that an earthquake preceeded the eruption of the volcano. Although we cannot know the exact time interval between the earthquake and the eruption we know that it must have been at least a year. Seeds, which were left on the ruins of the houses, had begun to germinate when the first ash fell. This means that the inhabitants had been forced to abandon their houses well before the volcano erupted. It explains why no skeletons of humans or animals (with the exception of a pig) have been found. What is more, people had the time to collect all their valuables: jewelry, seal-stones, most bronzes, even tools. It is clear therefore, that not only did they have plenty of time at their disposal, but that they got well organized for a mass migration. We know that they left Akrotiri, but as of yet, we have no idea where they went. Perhaps we will find evidence of their colony somewhere on the mainland or Crete. The earthquake was very destructive. It is responsible for the ruinous state of the houses that you see on the site because once ash began falling from the volcano, the houses were packed so well, that they escaped any further damage in the centuries to come. But why did the people leave? Usually they stay to rebuild their stricken town. We do not know the answer, but we can speculate. Perhaps some smoke from the volcano warned them that worse was to come. Perhaps their priests had dreams of warning and forced them to leave, much as Moses led his people through the desert. It seems, however, that some people lingered on in the ruins even after the majority of the population had left. Sp. Marinatos called them troglodytes (dwellers in the ruins). Ch. Doumas, who is carrying on the excavations now, thinks they were a team repairing the ruined buildings. These people managed to escape as well, because we have not found their skeletons. But we can infer their presence because things were moved around **on the ash and volcanic pumice,** a certain testimony that some humans were present at the time of the eruption.

The stairway of the N. facade of sector D.

Society

and

Religion

No written documents were found at Akrotiri yet; consequently our inferences about the society have to based on the archaeological material. This can be very revealing however. First of all we can tell that Akrotiri was a very wealthy town. Despite the systematic removal of all the valuables, the quality of the frescoes, the pottery and last but not least the magnificence of the buildings themselves testify to an important community. Several types of buildings can be distinguished. Isolated houses built with dressed ashlar stones, isolated houses built with mud brick, and blocks of dwellings. Clearly the architecture reveals something about the hierarchy of the society. The isolated buildings would be the dwellings of the more important officials. So far no palace has been discovered, therefore there existed no king. We must be cautious, however, because the excavation is far from being finished. In the very south of the settlement, just as the visitor enters, there must have existed the religious and administrative centre of the community. This can be deduced by the importance of the buildings most of them built in ashlar masonry. It is impossible to tell how many people lived in each building. By analogy with other cultures, we can suppose that the masters slept and lived in the upper storeys while the servants or workers slept down below. It is likely that the quarters of the latter were much more cramped, and many people slept even in the storage-rooms among the jars.

35. *A view of the magazines, sector A.*

An interesting point about the town is that we do not have industrial quarters, residential areas, suburbia, slums like in a modern city. Although there exists a concentration of industrial quarters on one area of the site (sector Γ), in most cases, we have the following picture: upper storeys are residential and ceremonial quarters, while the ground floors and basements are industrial quarters. Thus, we have a vertical, not a horizontal division in society. This surely has implications for our understanding of the nature of the social hierarchy. I suggest that industry and economy were controlled **per building.** As we shall see, the masters of these buildings were not just wealthy people but officiated as priests as well.

What kind of industry did there exist in the ground floors of the buildings? The most important were mills where the grain was ground into flour and was distributed to the people. It is not an accident that one mill was situated at a square so that people could come and procure the amount of flour which was probably alotted to them as payment. A broad door and window in the mill facilitated transactions (fig. **24**). We know that in Egypt, the pharaoh payed his subjects in kind for their services. It is very likely that the same was the case at Akrotiri.

Apart from mills, Akrotirians had metal work-shops, lapidary work-shops for the making of stone objects, pottery work-shops etc. Large storage areas or magazines existed as well, serving the needs of the

18. Rhyton resembling a bull with a net on its back.

23. Rhyton ressembling a lion's head.

19. Rhyton resembling a lion's head.

36. View of the magazines, sector A.

community rather than single family units. Such is the case with the N. magazines of sector A (fig. **35**)and with room B1 (fig. **1**). The communal magazines imply that some form of collective economy was operative at Akrotiri; more will be said about that later.

Regarding the people's diet, we can infer the following on the basis of the food remnants that have been found. Beans, lentils, pulses, bread, sheep, goats, deer, pigs were the vegetables, plants and animals which were consumed.

Their furniture was quite elaborate. Beds, stools and a nice table have been reconstructed on the basis of casts which were made from imprints that these furniture made on the ash. Otherwise wooden objects do not survive, of course.

Domestic arrangements are also in evidence. A few kitchens have been identified by the presence of hearths and cooking pots. What is significant in this context, is that the kitchens in question do not appear to have belonged to a single household but rather to a community of families. This can be deduced by the presence of several cooking pots and conical cups (which would have served as plates) in a single room. (fig. **2**). The cooking pots and cups are so numerous, that one simply has to infer communal meals.

The subject of religion has been one of my main concerns. This is because religion is everywhere in evidence: in the pottery, in the fres-

coes, in the architecture. Very much of the pottery is cultic in character and we can identify it on the basis of Cretan equivalents. The most common type is a conical vase called **rhyton** which was used for libations (liquid offerings to the deity). Another form of rhyton or libation vase has the form of an animal, a bull or a lion (figs **18, 19, 23**). The reason is that many animals were sacred to the gods and were often sacrificed to them. Other cultic equipment comprises tables of offerings, which are low tables on which one could place bloodless offerings to the divinity. This cultic equipment is found in many rooms at Akrotiri. Some of these rooms were simple storage areas or treasuries, but others were painted with frescoes. The latter rooms were undoubtedly shrines where rituals were performed. These shrines are always associated with industrial quarters or with kitchens. For example there was a shrine above the storage room B1 (fig. **1**) and the kitchen room B2 (fig. **2**). There was also a shrine associated with one of the mills. This can mean one thing: the priests were in charge of the economic activities at Akrotiri and the society was theocratic (dominated and operated by religious institutions). Thus, the priests would have formed the elite, the aristocracy of society. They would have controlled trade and production. They would have amassed wealth which they would use for the embelishment of the town but also to pay the people who worked for them. The craftsmen, the artists, the scribes would all have had to be supported. The model which I propose might sound strange to modern ears, but it was the accepted way of life in the contemporary civilizations of the Near East. There also, economy was controlled by the temple, if not by the king.

What kinds of gods did the Akrotirians worship? Here it is very difficult to give an answer. It is impossible to penetrate the minds of people who lived several thousands of years ago and to visualize their beliefs, if we have no written records. All we have is pictures, their frescoes. We also know that their religion was similar to that of contemporary Minoan Crete because the Cretans used the same type of cult equipment and painted the same types of frescoes. Looking at the religious evidence from both Akrotiri and Crete, we can deduce the following: A lot of the cult was related to fertility and vegetation. We can be sure of this because the frescoes often depict scenes of nature, while vegetation is the most frequent motif on their pottery. (figs. **4, 7, 9**). One type of pot (fig. **22**), which must have been a cult vessel, deserves special attention because of its obvious connotations of fertility. It has an anthropomorphic shape, resembling a woman, with breasts, earrings and sometimes necklaces. Not infrequently, these types of pots which are called «Breasted ewers», have plant motifs painted on them. There can be no clearer indication of the associations of fertility with a female divinity. In fact, the Minoan goddess is often depicted on frescoes or

5. Ewer with a bird decoration.

The breasted ewer with the barley. It was of a religious use and it is a typical example of the Cycladic art.

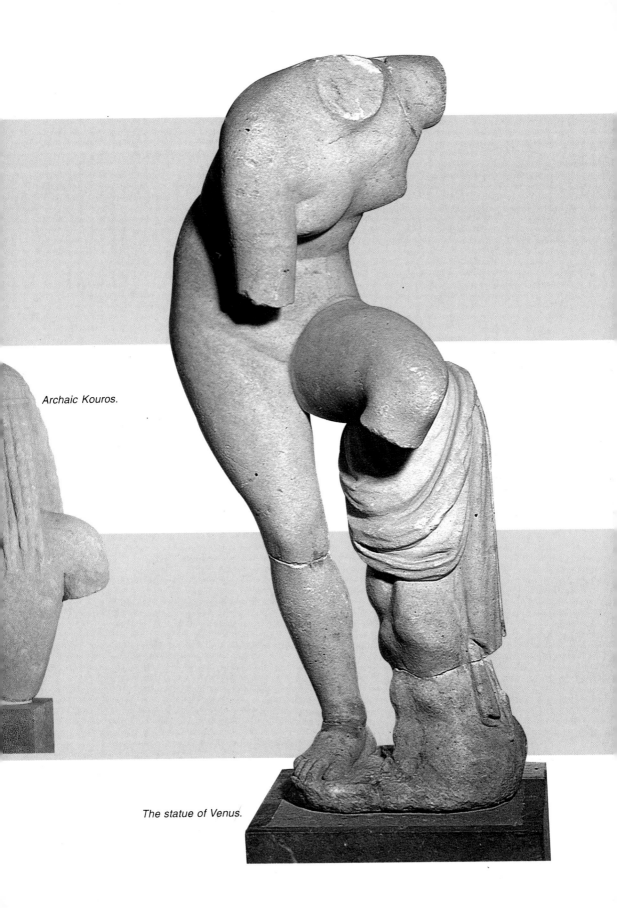

Archaic Kouros.

The statue of Venus.

on seal-stones. She is also depicted on a fresco from Akrotiri, which is not yet published, and where she sits on a platform flanked by a griffin and a monkey. Were there any male gods? Here scholars disagree and some want to see a society dominated only by women. This is very unlikely, however. Male priests certainly existed as well, and it is hardly imaginable that male gods are completely absent in any religion. Thus, although Minoan and Akrotirian religion seems to put more emphasis on the goddess of fertility, male gods are not to be excluded. Animals were important for the religion of these people. Monkeys and horned

27. Rhyton resembling an ostrich egg.

animals (bulls, deer, goats, antelopes) as well as lions were thought of as special companions of the gods. This is why they often feature on religious representations either together with the goddess or guarding her shrine. The animals also appear in the form of **rhyta** (offering vessels) which are very charming works of art as well as characteristic cult equipment (figs. **18, 19, 23**).

Because religion was, to a great extent, concerned with fertility, flowers played a great role in the lives of the Akrotirians. Lilies, crocuses, ivy and papyrus plants are frequently depicted on frescoes (fig. **28, 29**) and on the pottery (figs. **7, 9**).

Judging from the architectural evidence, the Akrotirians had no detached temples of the form that we find in Egypt, the Near East or even later Greece. Rather, they had small-scale shrines which were incorporated in buildings which served a variety of functions. Thus, we may assume that in a given building there existed a shrine, an industrial sector, magazines for storage and living quarters. Although the building was principally the residence of the priests, we cannot call it a temple because its principal function was not to house the cult image of the deity. According to historians of religion, we must use the word temple only if the cult, which took place there, was centered around the cult image of the god. But at Akrotiri we have found no traces of cult images. It is true that had they existed, the inhabitants would have carried

10. Offering table.

26. Copper utensils, probably pans.

them away. However, we have found no suitable architectural arrangement such as a platform or a niche in which the presumed cult image would have stood.

To return to the shrines at Akrotiri. There were many, as I have already mentioned, corresponding to the number of buildings and blocks. They were all painted with frescoes. They were small, so that only a few priests could perform the required rituals in them. But was there no large place for public worship? Were the common people barred from cult? This of course is not the case. We know that public worship took

place out in the open, in the fields, in caves, on top of the mountains. From Crete we have both pictorial and archaeological evidence to confirm this, and given the similarity between Akrotirian and Cretan (Minoan) religion, we have every reason to believe that the same was the case with Akrotiri. Thus, the shrines in the settlement served only as the focus of the religious administration. The priests performed the necessary rituals there, but they were also responsible for the economy and wellfare of the community.

The shrines may have been associated with different festivals which were crucial for the entertainment of the people and which acted as cohesive forces in society, much as Christmas or Easter function for us. These festivals, to which the frescoes allude, included a harvest or spring festival (fig. **14**), a marine festival (fig. **13**), initiation festivals for the younger members of the community (fig. **19**) etc. Many of them, in fact almost all, took place outdoors with a large number of spectators watching.

13. The fresco of the Marine Festival.

17. The fresco of the river.

Relations with Crete

One of the interesting points which emerged from the excavations of Akrotiri, was the similarity of its art and architecture with Minoan Crete. Crete was at the peak of her culture at that time around 1500 B.C. She apears to have had a powerful fleet with which she dominated the sea, the so-called **Minoan Thalassocracy.** For this reason, some scholars supposed that Akrotiri was, in fact, a Minoan colony serving trade purposes. This is not the case however. Akrotiri was built many

29. The fresco of the spring. Detail from the northern wall. Flirting swallows.

centuries before it became Minoanized, and many of its architectural features have a strong Cycladic flavour. It is clearly not a colony but a Cycladic town which is **strongly minoanized.** The pottery is imitating Minoan pottery, the great buildings copy Minoan architectural features, the frescoes are painted in the Minoan tradition with Minoan subjects. Most of all, **the religion is Minoan.** All this requires an explanation. Could it be that the influence is only superficial? For example, Europe is very Americanized today if we judge from jeans, coca cola, hamburgers, American TV programmes and movies and many other items. Still, European culture has not merged with the American one, and certainly Europe is not militarily dominated by the USA. Some scholars think that this is the case with Akrotiri. Minoan influence does not mean domination but simply a cultural influence. But this does not explain why Minoan religion was taken over. I believe that the Minoans brought Santorini into their sphere of influence **through religion itself.** Was that not what the Jesuits did in China and Japan in the 16th century? By proselytizing these people into Christianity they were able to build a formidable economic empire. In conclusion, Akrotiri was under the sphere of influence of Crete, an influence that was exerted through religion. It was not a Minoan colony, however.

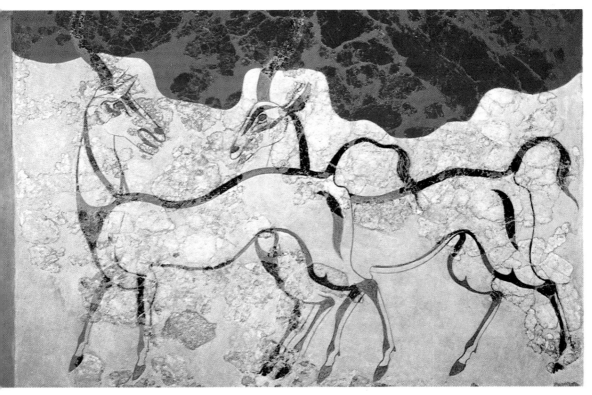

20. *The fresco of the antelopes (oryx beissa).*

The Frescoes

Most of the Akrotiri frescoes are on exhibit in the National Museum in Athens. They all depict scenes of a religious content although this is hard for the modern spectator to understand. But art in this period was functional, it served a purpose. It expressed the official ideology of the society, an ideology which was either political or religious or a mixture of both. In this case we have no political propaganda as in Egypt where the person of the pharaoh is depicted in many places and in many forms, we have only religious art.

Fresco of the Ladies (figs. **11, 12**). These are only two fragments from a larger composition which depicted a series of ladies, dressed in elaborate dresses and wearing earrings and other jewelry. They were most probably carrying gifts to a seated goddess (?) or a shrine. In the background of these ladies, there were papyrus plants, which are sacred plants to the divinity.

11, 12. Frescoes: from the house of the Ladies.

Fresco of Papyrus Plants (fig. **28**). This is from the same composition as the ladies mentioned above. Papyrus plants grow in Egypt and were taken over by the Minoans and Akrotirians from there. They are most probably sacred plants like the lilies and crocuses.

Spring Fresco with Lilies. From D2 (figs. **14, 29**). The painting depicts lilies growing in a rocky landscape. The colours are almost an impressionistic rendering of light reflected on the rocks. The red and brown rocks are reminiscent of the Akrotiri landscape of today. The lilies, growing from these rocks are not static. The Minoan artist avoided monotony at all costs, so he made them bend slightly, thus giving the

28. The fresco of the papyrus. From the house of the Ladies.

impression of a breeze. The lily flowers are depicted in all the phases of their life: buds, just opening flowers, and fully opened flowers. Swallows are courting in the air. This animates the painting and, at the same time, tells you what it is all about: the coming of the Spring.

The Ship fresco (fig. **13**). This was part of a frieze which was set above the windows of room **5** in the «West House». It depicts a fleet returning to a home port. Although the excavator originally assumed that the fleet was returning from an expedition, another interpretation seems better. A religious-military festival is shown, which perhaps commemorated a victory of the Therans over their enemy. The procession of ships celebrates this victory in a festival which is a thanksgiving to the deity. The religious character of the procession can be deduced from the special adornments of the ships especially the leading one (to the right of the picture, fig. **13**). It should be noted that crocus flowers hang from the festoons. Also the ships are not rowed but paddled, an impractical method if the journey is to be imagined as a long one. Most probably it was only a short trip from one island town to Akrotiri itself. The military character can be deduced from the presence of helmets and spears which hang from the cabins of the captains of the ships. Finally the lions, which are emblems on the sides of some ships, definitely denote aggression. In this context one should note also the lion chasing a deer on the left of the picture, the purpose of which is to reinforce the theme of aggression.

The Tropical Landscape (fig. **17**). It is a frieze which run across the E wall of room **5** of the West House. It should be understood in connection with the ship procession fresco above. It depicts two predatory animals an imaginary one, a griffin (lion with eagle's head) and a wild

14. The room with the spring fresco.

16. Cabin Screen Fresco.

30. The fresco of the young priestess from the west house.

15. The fresco of the blue monkeys.

cat hunting near a river. The palms suggest a tropical landscape, and some have thought that it depicts a concrete place in Libya or the East. However, the presence of the imaginary animal, the griffin, suggests that this is only a genre scene, the purpose of which is to show **aggression**. As we have seen hunting is present also in the ship fresco symbolized by the lion emblems of the ships as well as the hunting lion on the landscape to the upper left of the ship fresco. Thus, the two friezes together allude to hunting and aggression.

The Fisherman (fig. **25**). There were in fact two very similar frescoes of «fishermen» set in two corners of the same room where the ship fresco was found. The fish establish a thematic link with the marine festival of the ship fresco. Although the men are usually called fishermen, they are special servants of the deity. This can be argued because of two special features which characterize them: their partially shaved head and their nudity. Minoan males are never shown in the nude unless in the act of adoration: the god had to see you in all your purity. Therefore, the frescoes depict two adorants who are in the act of offering fish. An offering table depicting fish, has been found in the corner where the adorants would meet, if they walked (compare with fig. **10**)

The Priestess (fig. **30**). Found in room **4** of the West House the woman is undoubtedly a priestess because of her unusual attire. She is wearing a kind of sari, and on her head she has a tight-fitting blue cap on which a snake is sewn. The snake could have been made of cloth or leather. Snakes on headdresses of priestesses or goddesses are well known from Crete. She is holding a vase with a long handle of a type that is attested archaeologically. It is not certain what was contained in it. Some have said there were burning coals, others cakes. I wonder if it is not red pigment which she has just applied on herself. Note her vivid red lips and red-painted ear which is surely a ritual adornment. It is interesting that red pigment in a broken bowl was found in the room of the priestess.

The Cabin-Screen Fresco (fig. **16**). It was found in room **4** of the West House next to room **5** of the adorant fishermen and the ship fresco (figs. **25, 13**). It cannot be understood out of context because it depicts the cabin-screen of the leader of the fleet of the ship fresco (fig. **13**). Here you see only one example; in reality, there were found seven to eight of these frescoes all depicting similar, but not identical, cabin-screens. This has a special significance, namely it connects the room, in which the fresco was found, with the leader of the fleet. Sp. Marinatos thought that this was the admiral's room, but since the ship-fresco shows a religious procession with a military character, the leader of the fleet must have had some religious function as well. Indeed this is shown by the stylized lilies which adorn the top of the poles. It will be remembered that lilies are sacred flowers to the divinity. We must imagine the cabins as made of animal hides attached to wooden poles.

The Monkeys (fig. **15**). The composition is, to a large extent, restored out of incomplete fragments, but the subject is clear: monkeys climbing on rocks in an animated fashion. The rocks are rendered schematically, but the monkeys are very life-like. This is the strength of the Minoan painters that they render such convincing pictures of nature, especially animals. What the rest of the composition depicted, we do not know, but monkeys are often shown as special servants of the deity. On an unpublished fresco from Akrotiri, a monkey touches the goddess, whereas on another he is shown in front of an altar.

The Antelopes (fig. **20**). We see here only one pair of antelopes which are so realistically rendered, that we can identify the species: Oryx Beissa. There were actually six antelopes painted in the room, two pairs and two single ones. They are painted in simple outline but with a marvelously convincing effect. They are probably not courting as was originally suggested. They seem to belong to the same sex because they have the same size. I believe they are engaged in playful competition as young animals are prone to do in the spring. The ivy border above them also suggests spring-time activity.

The Boxing Children (fig. **21**). They come from the same room as the antelopes and there is a thematic link between these compositions. The children are engaged in playful activity and competition just as the antelopes are. They are not ordinary children but special servants of the deity because they have partially shaved heads. One of them wears also jewelry, earrings, a necklace and bracelets. Given the fact that athletic contests were always connected with some religious festival in antiquity (like the Olympic games of Classical Greece were performed in the honour of Zeus), it is a religious festival that is depicted here. The mood is cheerful and a kind of **joie de vivre** dominates both compositions.

25. The fresco of the adorant.

21. The fresco of the boxing children.

The Pottery

and

Other Vessels

Of the hundreds of pots that have been discovered at Akrotiri, some characteristic samples only are available for the visitor. One can divide the pottery and other vessels in the following categories: **Bronze Jugs and pans.** These are rare because most were taken away by the inhabitants, but what remains gives us a glimpse of the high technology of the Aegean bronze smiths (figs. **26**).

Cook-ware: These are usually coarse pottery and comprise cooking pots, ovens and stands for spits. On fig. **2** you can see many cooking pots as they were found in a room.

Grinding vessels and Mortars. They are made of stone and represent the most ordinary, low quality vessels that you find in Akrotiri. They were used for grinding and pounding various substances ranging from corn to pigments.

Jugs. The majority of the vases are jugs painted mostly with floral motifs (figs. **4, 7, 9**) although some have birds (fig. **5**). The floral motifs are copied from Cretan pottery and are connected with the idea of fertility and vegetation which we meet constantly in Minoan and Akrotirian art. A special category are the **nippled ewers** (fig. **3**) which allude to fertility and the female goddess. Many of the jugs are imported from Crete as we can tell from their lustrous surface (fig. **8**). Nippled ewers, however, represent a local tradition and they are always locally made.

8. Imported ewer with spiral decoration.

9. Flower-vase with white lilies.

7. Ewer with beautifully shaped eyes and a decoration of branches of myrtle and flowers.

6. Pithos (storage jar) with rope decoration.

3. Breasted ewer.

4. Ewer with a floral decoration.

22. Breasted ewer.

31. Akrotiri complex D.

Flower pots. Some vases appear to have had no practical function, and they seem to have been constructed solely for the purpose of holding flowers. Such is the vase of fig. **9.**

Tables of Offering (fig. **10**). Tripod low tables of circular form have been found in some numbers at Akrotiri. They are found in shrines. The one of fig. **10** is painted with dolphins. Two of such a type were found in the West House together with the frescoes, all of which allude to a marine festival.

Pithoi or Storage Jars (fig. **6**). They vary in size and decoration, but were all used for storage of liquids and other substances such as flour, honey etc. The one of fig. **6** has a rope decoration imitating real ropes that were sometimes tied around the storage jars.

24. Installation of a mill in Akrotiri.

32. Prof. Spyridon Marinatos in the mill.

Guide

to the

Antiquities

The first building you see to your left, as you approach the site and before your ticket is checked, is **XESTE 3.** It is one of the most grandiose buildings of the site built with ashlar masonry (dressed blocks) in its facade. It was used for ceremonial purposes because it contains many large rooms. The frescoes revolve around themes of vegetation, animals and the goddess. It included domestic or service rooms which are much smaller in size and which contained tools and storage jars. To the S. of the building you will note stone tools lying around. These belong to the people that were left behind after the destructive earthquake but before the eruption (see above, «The Earthquake and the Eruption»). They were obviously planning to repair the building but they never got that far.

After having entered the roofed area, you are walking on a street which runs N-S through the settlement. To the left you have **Sector Γ.** The industrial installations of the town are most evident there, although they are present in virtually every building. You will note many stone tools lying around, as well as troughs and mortars. In these rooms workers pounded and worked various substances and possibly repaired damages, as can be deduced from the presence of hammers and anvils.

To your right is **Sector B.** Note the small windows on the level of the street which gave access to light into the basement and workshops of this sector. Tree-truncs were inserted in the walls (now restored with gypsum) to give them more elasticity and render them earthquake resistant. As you proceed northwards, you will reach a small square. Facing you is a mill. The bench on which the miller sat, and the clay bucket in which he poured the flour, are still in situ (figs. **24, 32**). Through the large door of the mill, distribution of flour would take place to the people gathered in the square. Across from the mill and to the south is room B1 of sector B. It is the room of the **Antelopes and Boxing Children,** and it was a shrine because it contained a small treasury with cultic equipment. Note the large window facing the square where the priests could have appeared for the public to see. Thus the square serves a double purpose, one secular (flour distribution) and one religious.

Moving on to the North, you will reach another square (fig. **33**) larger than the first. This is dominated by the **West House** (fig. **34**). It has irregular windows because symmetry was not strictly observed, nor was it such an important aesthetic ideal as later. Its most interesting feature is the large window. I believe it was a window of appearances

as the previous one of B1. Indeed the fresco of the priestess (fig. **30**), the adorants carrying fish (fig. **25**) as well as the ship fresco frieze were found in this building. We may imagine that the priestess appeared from the window to the people below. The West House was evidently a «cult centre» with a shrine above and industrial quarters below. A kitchen, a metallurgy workshop, grinding stones and storage jars were found in the groundfloor. Here economy and religion are combined in a characteristic manner.

While you are in the square, you can look through the windows of **sector D,** which is to your right as you are facing the West House. You will see a typical basement with storage jars and other pottery. Some pieces of furniture, including a table were recovered from there. If you continue to the North, you will pass the «**House of the Ladies**» on your left. There, the frescoes with the Ladies and the Papyruses (figs. **11, 12, 28**) were found. It contained also rich store-rooms and a lapidary's workshop: an unfinished marble vase was found in this building.

The most Northern building **Sector A** is a big store-room. It had three rooms in a row, containing many storage jars and big windows for distribution purposes. (figs. **35, 36**). Thus, it was a communal magazine. Next to it was a mill, whereas on the upper storey, there existed another shrine.

Now you start going South, to look at the **region East of the street.**

You will be looking at **sectors D and B** from the other side. Note that these are blocks, not isolated buildings. Each unit had a shrine. Room D2 was the shrine of the Lilies where the fresco with the same name was found (fig. **14**). There was also the shrine of the Antelopes and Boxing Children, mentioned above, and the shrine with the Monkey fresco (fig. **15**). Industrial quarters, kitchens, mills and storage areas are distributed in these sectors, and they are always close to shrines. A mill-stone was found next to the Lilies shrine, a storage room was below the Antelope and Boxing children shrine (figs. **20, 21**) etc. Note the impressive Eastern facade of sector D standing three storeys high (fig. **31**).

Fira

The town of Fira stands out like a white eagles'-nest, hanging between sea and sky. The climb from the bay to the town can be made on foot for those who want to try their strength, climbing the 600 steps of the road, or with the cable railroad. There also are good-natured donkeys, who offer their backs to those who want to enjoy the experience of donkey-riding. Their pack-saddles are decorated with blankets of many colours, "kilimia", and the coloured beads on their harnesses give a unique and joyful colour, which is still maintained on an island which is fighting to keep its local colour and its folk personality.

The capital of the island was moved to Fira from Pyrgos Kallistis in the beginning of the 19th century. Now Fira is a growing town with a population of about

1500 people, which lives in the present but tries to retain the local traditions of the past.

In the summer, a loud and good-natured crowd of people strolls, carefree, on the roads which are parallel to the cliff and the small streets that cross them. The central part of the town, the market, is here. Numerous shops offer a great variety of merchandice, satisfying even the most demanding customers. Also, the offered merchandice, from the cheapest (cotton shirts and blouses) to the most expensive (furs and jewelry) give it a particular accent which is quite interesting to the visitor. The visit to the picturesque market of Fira is a pleasant walk. Small houses, dug in the land, one- or two-storied, have a view of either the sea or the land. Lit and crowded against each other, as they are, on the top of the cliff, they seem to be wanting to support each other, so they can reach outward, over the abyss. Terraces of houses which are not terraces but balconies or passages, vaults and archways, and small, white, decorated facades. Straight lines are unknown, everything is in

The harbour. This is where the stepped road starts. It leads to the capital of the island, Thera.

Panoramic view of the town Fira.

curves, giving a unique architectural characteristic to the houses of Fira which are sunk inside the earth. "Skafta" (dug) as the locals call them, they are built from stone and the earth of the island.

Do not wonder if, when passing through the door of a building which is, at first glance, one-storied, you walk many steps down and yet do not end in some dank and dark basement, but, when you open your window, you see the sea reflecting the sun, although you have descended two or three storeys inside the earth.

At Fira, buildings do not have height, they have depth.

The Archaeological Museum

Of the town of Fira features collections from the excavations of Mesa Vouno, where Ancient Thera and the Sellada cemetery are, from Akrotiri, and various utensils from other areas. Amphoras, pottery, earthen casks, marble Kouroi, female statuettes, coins, etc. are sheltered in the halls of the museum. These collections cover a long period, which starts in the third millenium B.C. and ends in the Roman years.

Churches

Fira is the seat for both an Orthodox and a Catholic bishop. The Metropolitan church of Ypapanti was built on 1827 by Marko Belonias, and that is why it is called "Panaghia of Belonia". The original building was destroyed by the earthquakes of 1956 (July 9). In its place a new church, Metamorphosis, was built. There also are the Catholic church and the Convent of the Dominican Order.

The visit to the old mansions and houses of the town is interesting. Among the mansions, Gyzi's, an authentic building of the Venetian years, stands out. Today it belongs to the Catholic church of the island. It has been restored and is used for various cultural meetings. The building houses an impressive collection of antiques, furniture, engravings, and other art objects from centuries past.

The Convent of St. Nickolas

Is the oldest convent of the island. It was built in its present position on 1815-20. Originally, the convent had been built in inaccesible Skaros, but the nuns moved it from the ruined castle of Skaros to its present position. The Gyzis family had a private temple in impassable Skaros, dedicated to the memory of St. Nicholas. On 1651, the family got permission from the Bishop to convert the small church to a convent. The girls of the Gyzis family became the first nuns. The convent became property of the Greek state on 1849.

In the center of the convent's courtyard, there is the handsome triune church of St. Nicholas. The 32 cells of the nuns are in the buildings around the church. The attention of the visitor is drawn to the temple screen and the old icons.

Firostefani

It's a small, elongated village, very near Fira, which seems more like a neighborhood of Fira than a separate village. Among the sights of the village are the churches of Aghios Minas and Aghios Georgios.

The view of the volcano and the caldera are panoramic. The most picturesque part of the village is its rebuilt part, which is next to the edge of the cliff. The Catholic church is also interesting. The Catholic's area, the "Frangika", is located between Fira and Firostefani. The convents of the Dominicans and the Sisters of Mercy are there. Also, the Lazarists founded there the Greco-French school of St. Joseph.

Imerovigli
or
Merovigli

As the locals call it, is very near, about 1km. N.W. of the village of Firostefani. Its location near the edge of the cliff, its name, of the day-Vigla, as well as the time when it was built, show that during the years of the pirates' attacks it had been a daily observatory. The Viglator -guard-watched the sea, and, if pirates appeared, apprised the population of the approaching danger. Most old buildings are ruined. The church of Panaghia Malteza is interesting. It is called Malteza (Maltese) because the icon of the Virgin was found on the port of Malta by a Santorinian captain and carried to Imerovigli, where the captain built a church for it.

Skaros

Majestic Skaros rises perpendicularly to the coast, on the most northern end of the area. The medieval capital of Santorini was built in an inaccesible and unapproachable area. The castle was built by a Roman noble named Scaurus, who was governor of the island when it was possessed by the Romans. The castle, built on top of a steep, dark, and dreadful crag, was one of the five medieval castles of the island, seat of the Venetian Archons and of the Catholic bishops. The remains of the castle and the ruins of the Venetian buildings are discernible. Ancient ruins and graves have been found in the area.

The church of Theoskepasti ("God-covered") is interesting. The church was built by a seaman who believed that he was saved from a great storm with the Virgin's help. Most of the 352 churches of Santorini have been built by seamen whose patron Saint saved them from storms or other great dangers.

Vourvoulos

The village Vourvoulos, the village of the mule-guides of Santorini, is located east of Imerovigli. Most Santorinian mule-guides are descended from this village. In the area Kato Vourvoulos we find the wonderful church of St. Panteleimon.

Foinikia

Lies about 9km. from Fira. Good roads and regular transportation connect this village with the capital of the island. Foinikia, Oia, and Tholos, with its few houses, are the villages of north Santorini, the Upper Side, as the locals call it. Foinikia is a representative traditional Santorinian village. Houses built with the traditional ways, harmoniously attached to each other, present a wonderful totality of traditional architecture. A black stone wall rises like a fence near the entrance of the village. In the Gonia region there is an archaeological site.

Oia

The distance that separates Oia from Fira is not over 10km. of paved road. The small houses, carved into the rock, the mansions with their stairways and their neoclassical architecture, with white and ochra as their dominant colours, the walls decorated with small stones, the roads paved with flagstones, and the flowers, form a harmonious total of the impressive picture of the village. The village square is a balcony looking at the caldera. The view of the volcano and the infinity of the sea take a different dimension when seen from here. The wealth of the villagers of the last century is exhibited in the Nautical museum of Oia. Oia's inhabitants were sailors, and became rich in the last century by working in the sea. They decorated their village with neoclassical buildings which today bear witness to an age that has passed.

The church of Aghiou Sozontos (Saviour) was built before 1680. The sunset will be not forgotten by those who enjoy it.

BEACHES There are two beaches in the Oia area. The access is difficult though, as they cannot be reached by car. One can only go on foot. If someone wants to go to the **"Armeni"** beach, where the harbour is, he should descend about 300 steps. The road to **"Ammoudi"** beach has about 200 steps. A good road is the one that goes to the huge beach of the **"Baxedes"** area. This area is about 3km. away from Oia. Near the back side of the village is **"Katharos"** beach. There is a country infirmary in Oia.

The explosion period was called the "Bad Time" by the inhabitants. When peace and quiet were reestablished, the locals built the church of Panaghia tou Kalou ("Virgin of the Good") on the Koloumba site. In the cape area there are images carved on the rocks, They are the so-called "cells". These images, carved on the rocks, are inscriptions with the names of gods and heroes, and are characteristic of Santorini.

BEACHES An extended beach, perfect for enjoying the sea, starts from Cape Kolumbo and continues till Cape Exomytis. As an indication we'll mention the Pori, Kanakari, and Exo Yalou beaches and other areas.

Koloumbos

The other volcano of Santorini, the crater of which is underwater. Its distance from Fira is about 20km. The volcano's eruption on 1650 A.D. was quite strong. It was accompainied by earthquakes, tidal waves, and poisonous gases. Areas near Perissa and Kamari were flooded, and ancient ruins came to the surface when the waters receded. The sound of the explosion was heard at Chios, and the coasts of Asia Minor were covered by a thin layer of ash. The tidal wave reached Crete.

The famous beach at Ammoudi (Ia).

Karterados

The village is east of Fira, at a distance of less than 2km. The architecture of the village's houses is interesting. The church of Analipsis is worth seeing.

Mesaria

The village is about 4km. distant from Fira, to the S.E. This beautiful village of Santorini is surrounded by vineyards and gardens. Mesaria is a production center of the famous Santorinian wine. The village churches of Metamorphosis tou Soteros and Aghia Irini were built between 1680 and 1700.

Monolithos

This typical village of Santorini is near the island's airport. It lies about 7km. from Fira. An organized beach is in operation there.

The village of Mesaria.

Monolithos: The beach.

Episkopi

Gonias

In the area of the village Mesa Gonia, which is about 6km. distant from Fira and very near Kamari, Episkopi Gonias, a church dedicated to the Assumption of the Virgin, is located. The church is of the Byzantine style, cross-shaped, with a cupola and ante-temple. It was built in the end of the 11th century, with all expenses paid by the Byzantine emperor Alexios Komnenos. Large tracts of land were given to the church by imperial warrant.

Today, the building we see is altered by additions. Certain examples of Byzantine hagiography of the 11th century have been preserved on the arches of the church. The marble screen of the temple is intact. The church was the seat of the bishop of Thera. After the island was occupied by the Venetians on 1207, the Orthodox bishop was driven out, and the expulsion was followed by the installation of a Catholic bishop. When Santorini was occupied by the Turks on 1537, a new dispute started between Catholics and Orthodox. The long clash between the two docrines caused the intervention of the Patriarch of Constantinople. The Orthodox Patriarch, with the Turkish Sultan concurring, ceded the possession of the temple to the Orthodox, and divided the property of the church equally among the two docrines. The Patriarchal decision of 1614 ended the clash and restored peace among the two Christian communities and the clergy that represented them.

The village of Episkopi Gonias.

Kamari

A modern tourist village, continually evolving. About 10km. distant from Fira in a S.W. direction. A sight of the village is the church of Myrtidiotissa. Many ancient artifacts have been found in the area. Ancient Oia, the port of the ancient capital of Thera, was here. A road connects Kamari with the archaeological site of ancient Thera.

The area has a beach many kilometers long. It is made of black sand and pebbles. The enjoyment of sun and sea has no limits.

Ancient Thera

The ancient capital of Thera. It is located on the S.W. part of the island, 15km. S.E. from Fira or 10km. S.E. from Kamari, built on a rocky slope of Mesa Vouno, at an elevation of 350 meters. The length of the ancient city (archaeological site) is not more than 800m., while its width approaches 200m. The archaeological site, the way it is shaped now, is an oblong area traversed by a central road and its branches.

The German archaeologist Hiller V. Gaertingen excavated the area during 1895-1903, on his own expense, and brought to light the ancient capital of Thera, the city of the mythical King Theras.

The city of Thera was the center of the island for a whole millenium. The buildings, the temples, the vases, the pottery, and the coins that have been found, record accurately the thousand-year long history of the island, from the age of the Dorians to the age of the Roman Empire.

The choice of location must have not been random. It may be connected to the defensive needs of the inhabitants of the island during the first millenium B.C. This interpretation is supported by the partly preserved strong walls that surrounded the city.

A road paved with flagstones led from the capital to its port, ancient Oia (today's Kamari). A visit to the archaeological site may start from Fira, Kamari, or Perissa. The excavations that took place along the road between ancient Thera and Kamari brought to light tombs of the Hellenistic and Palaeochristianic periods, which were hewn into the rock. The various artifacts found there, including clay vases, pottery, and gravestones, are ex-

hibited in the Archaeological Museum of Fira.

If we enter the ancient city from the left side, we see the small Byzantine church of Aghios Stephanos. This small church was built in the place where the palaeochristianic church of the Archangel Michael stood, as a marble inscription on the left wall informs us. Following the ancient road south, we meet the temple of the hero Artemidoros, an admiral of the Ptolemies. Engraved on the rocks are inscriptions, holy animals, the Ptolemaean eagle, the lion of Apollo, and Neptune's dolphins. Above and to the right of the dolphins, the head of Artemidoros is discernible. The symbols of the Dioscuri, Hecate, and Priapos are also distinguishable. Following the road to the edge of the city, we reach the church of Evangelismos tis Theotokou ("Annunciation of the Virgin"). The tomb of some hero is next to the church. From here, following the uphill road, we reach the archaic temple of Apollo Karneios. A temple of the Doric style, without an external collonade, with a court and a room for the priest, a portico, a sanctuary, and two small shrines. An external doorway is preserved. On the walls and rocks a large number of names of gods is discernible, written in the ancient Theran alphabet of the 7th century B.C. Next to the temple there is something resembling a raised court or terrace ("doma"), where the "orcheiseis" (dances) took place when the Dorians honored the god Apollo

on his 9 day long festival, the "Karneia". S.E. of the temple we find the Gymnasium of the Epheboi, a building of the 2nd century B.C. Here we also find inscriptions praising the manners and the customs of the Dorians. The holy cavern of Hermes and Heracles is located here. There are the remains of a bath near the west side of the Gymnasium. Following the main road of the city towards its center, we see the remains of private residences right and left. The Agora is located on the center of the city. On its west side we find the Vasiliki Stoa (Royal Portico), a Roman building, very probably of the reign of Augustus. It had an internal collonade of 12 columns which supported the roof of the building, and a separate space for the statues of the imperial family. Next to the portico is a small temple of the Hellenistic period dedicated to the worship of Dionysos. At this temple, during the reign of Augustus, the emperor was worshipped. To the south of the Agora the ruins of the city's theater, of the Hellenistic period, are preserved. The theater was also used for assemblies. During the reign of Caligula, statues of his mother Agrippina, as Hestia Voulaia, and of his father Germanicus, as Zeus Voulaios, had been erected there. West of the theater a Hellenistic building with a column-supported court may have been used as a place of assembly for the religious cult of the "Valistes", who worshipped the King.

The temple of Pythios Appolo, which was later converted to a Christian church, is behind the house of the Valistes. Also the temples of the Egyptian deities Isis, Serapis, and Anubis. To the N.W. side of the city are the "barracks" and the "Gymnasium" of the Ptolemies. Among others, private residences, hot baths, and a temple of Ptolemy III have been uncovered.

A little to the north there is an ancient temple which was converted to a Christian church, the Sotiras tou Christou ("Christ Saviour"). It is also called Christoulaki (Little Christ). Next to the church, in a natural cavern, there are the temples of Demetra and Persephone.

The cemetery of the ancient city is found in the Sellada area, a pass of Mesa Vouno. In the location Plagiades, on the N.E. side of the pass, 7th century B.C. tombs have come to light, with important funeral gifts. Another cemetery has been uncovered on the S.W. side of Mesa Vouno. The excavations, which started on 1895 and are still continuing, keep bringing to the surface artifacts from an age that was considered all but mythological a few years ago.

Temenos of Artemidoros.

Vothonas

Pyrgos

A village near Fira. The "dug" houses of the village are interesting, as well as the churches of Aghia Triada, Aghia Anna, and Panaghia, which was built on 1700. The church is "dug" at a height of about 20 meters from the ground, on a raised parapet called "trafos". It was used as a shelter by the people of Vothonas during attacks by pirates. After the people had climbed on the parapet, they pulled the wooden ladder. The twenty meters that separated them from the ground provided ample protection. The church is also known under the name Panaghia i Trypa (Virgin of the Crypt).

Located 8km. south of the town of Fira. The castle is built on the top of a round hill. The imposing settlement with its white picturesque buildings was the capital of the island till 1800. Tradition says that Pyrgos was one of the settlements of ancient Thera. Ruins of the medieval Venetian castle are preserved in the middle of the village. On top of the hill is the so-called Kasteli, which, with its beautiful view and its formation, is recommended for relaxation. The church of Theotokos, also called Theotokaki, a 10th century building, is also at Pyrgos. The chapel is the oldest medieval building of the area. The churches of the area are many, and all are of some interest, especially those built be-

fore 1650, as Aghia Theodosia, Taxiarchis Michael, and other saints of the Orthodox Church. A country infirmary is also there.

Profitis Ilias Monastery

The monastery of Profitis Ilias is located on the peak of the mountain of the same name, at a height of 550 meters. The monastery's construction was started on 1771 by the monks Joacchim and Gabriel. The two monks, with the permission and the help of the bishop of Thera, Zacharias, managed to obtain the sanction of the Patriarch of Constantinople, Cyril, to build the monastery. So, the newly founded monastery came under the spiritual protection of the Patriarchate and was titled a "Patriarchal Monastery". The building we see today is larger than the original. The monastery took its present form in the middle of the 19th century, when the King of Greece, Othon, visited Santorini. Othon was charmed by the landscape and urged that the monastery be expanded. The museum of the monastery is rich in ecclesiastical articles of inestimable value. Excepting the holy relics there, there are icons of the 15-18 centuries, gold-adorned vestments, the diamond-adorned mitre of the Patriarch Gregory E', silver-bound Scriptures, an iron cross of the 12th century (it is said that this cross was used by the Crusaders) and wood-carved ecclesiastical masterpieces.

The library of the monastery is impressive. It contains leather-bound books, hand-written Codexes, and various other ecclesiastical documents in many languages, as the five tomes of the New and Old Testament written by a son of Philip B' of Spain in Hebrew, Latin, and Greek. The leather-bound books alone number over 1200. The wood-carved temple screen of the church is impressive, as is the bell of the monastery. The monastery also contains a Folk Museum. This museum exhibits the tools of the various trades that the monks and the people of the island practiced. Complete workshops of the past century, fully equipped, seem to be waiting for the candle-maker, the barrel-builder, the blacksmith and the cobbler to start sweating in front of the bellows or the bench with the leather skins. The private Nomikos collection, which is housed in the

Monastery, includes embroidery, woven articles, and porcelain. The spiritual contribution of the monastery was limited, though, and cannot be compared to the activities of other monasteries. The only spiritual institution established by this monastery was some school in Pyrgos.

Athinios

The sole harbour of the island. The village has very old domed houses, dug in the volcanic rock, and these are the only sights worth seeing there.

A small beach, covered with pebbles, is good for swimming.

Megalochori

The village is about 9km. distant from Fira. Except for the churches of the Eisodia tis Theotokou and Aghioi Anargyroi, on the road to Emporio we find the church of Aghios Nicolaos Marmaritis. It is called Marmaritis because the whole building is made of marble ("marmaro"). This church was a pagan temple of the Doric style before the 4th century A.D. Its conversion to a Christian church left the original building of the 3rd century A.D. intact.

Akrotiri

A village in the S.W. part of the island, about 12km. distant from Fira. It is built on the most remote part of the island. The excavations in the area brought to light the settlement known as the City of Akrotiri.

It was one of the fortified castles of the island during the medieval years. After Santorini was occupied by the Turks, the strong Venetian castle was torn down. The remains of its towers are easily discernible. The old churches of Aghia Triada and Ypapanti tou Soteros are found in the area. From here, a road leads to the southern part of the island, where Faros is.

Emporio

A large village with a population of about 1000 people. It is built almost on the center of the plain, on a point which has a view towards both sides of the island. Small, picturesque streets and old mansions compose the beauty of the old village. It was one of the five areas of the island fortified with a castle during the Venetian years. Vestiges of the medieval castle (Mesana), which was equal to Pyrgos, remain till this day. North of the village, a bulky, square building, "Goulas", is located. It is a strong tower in which the people of the village found shelter and protection from the pirates. Tradition claims that this tower was built by monks from the Monastery of St. John in Patmos to protect the land and wealth of the monastery. The imposing church of Evangelismos is a modern building, built in the 1980's. To the right of the village, lining the hill, we see the picturesque windmills of Gavrilos.

The medieval castle Goulas at Emporio.

Perissa

A seaside settlement with a magnificent and interminable beach. The dark sea and the surrounding green make it one of the most beautiful on the island. The rocky bulk of Mesa Vouno, the remainder of ancient Aigiis, rises east of the village.

One of the island's largest churches, if not the largest, Timios Stavros ("Holy Cross") is located in Perissa. On the S.E. coast, not far from the village, is the monastery of Perissa. It is a 19th century building and has a five-domed church. The monastery was built on the ruins of the old church of Aghia Irini, which, it is believed, had given the island its name. But Aghia Irini itself had been built on the ruins of another, older church.

The famous beach at Perivolos.

Palaia
and
Nea Kameni

The two volcanic islands, where the crater of the volcano is. The visit to the volcano is made by boat. The whole area smells heavily of sulphur, while on many points the stones and earth are hot. The trip and the climb to the crater take about 1 1/2 hours.

Therasia

Small island opposite Oia. About one hour distant from Santorini. One can visit this small and barren island, with the few inhabitants, with an excursion boat. Its only sight is the wood-carved temple screen in the monastery Koimisis tis Theotokou. The screen was made in Russia and placed in the church on 1872. The coasts of the island are out of the way and the beaches very few. A road with 150 steps leads from the harbour to the village Manola, the largest settlement on the island. Other villages on the island are Potamos and Agrilia. On the south end of the island there is a submarine cave, called Trypiti, that has two entrances. On the north side of the island is the church of Aghia Irini, which lays claim to the honor of having changed Thera's name to Santorini together with Aghia Irini of Perissa.

There is a country infirmary on the island.